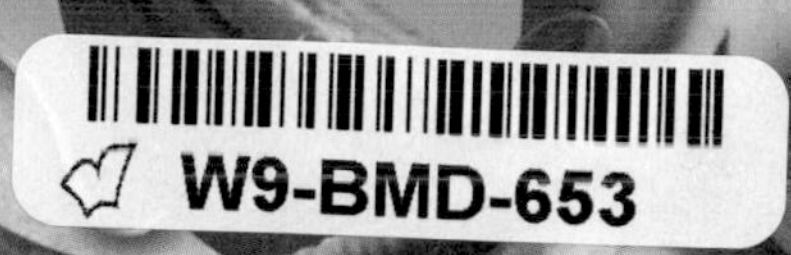

GROSS SCIENCE

by Paul Beck

SCHOLASTIC

an imprint of
SCHOLASTIC
www.scholastic.com

Published by Tangerine Press, an imprint of Scholastic Inc., 557 Broadway, New York, NY 10012; Scholastic Canada Ltd., Markham, Ontario; Scholastic Australia Pty. Ltd, Gosford NSW; Scholastic New Zealand Ltd., Greenmount, Auckland

Gross Science is produced by becker&mayer!, LLC.
11120 NE 33rd Place, Suite 101
Bellevue, WA 98004
www.beckermayer.com

If you have questions or comments about this product, please visit www.beckermayer/customerservice and click on Customer Service Request Form.

Edited by Ben Grossblatt
Designed by Tyler Freidenrich
Design assistance by Ryan Hobson and Megan Sugiyama
Photo illustrations by Ryan Hobson
Production assistance by Katie Stahnke and Rebecca Shapiro
Image research by Katie del Rosario
Production management by Jennifer Marx

Printed, manufactured, and assembled in Jefferson City, Missouri
First printing, November, 2011

12 11 10 9 8 7 6 5 4 3 2 1   11 12 13 14 15 16/0

ISBN: 978-0-545-38131-4

10480

Title page: Fly © jamesbenet/iStockphoto; banana © Prill Mediendesign & Fotografie/iStockphoto; worm © Dusty Cline/Dreamstime. Page 3: Torn paper © Uyen Le/iStockphoto. Page 4: Asparagus © Junyan Jiang/Dreamstime; water glass © Jakub Pavlinec/Shutterstock; toilet © aguirre_mar/iStockphoto. Page 5: Benjamin Franklin © Vladyslav Starozhylov/Dreamstime; sulfur © Robert Kyllo/iStockphoto; eggs © Alvin Teo © Dreamstime; graph paper © Tolimir/iStockphoto. Page 6: Orange bowl © Nikolay Pozdeev/iStockphoto; dish soap © Maria Toutoudaki/iStockphoto; pot of water © Foodmaniac/Dreamstime. Page 7: Tablespoon of white sugar © Marek Uliasz/Dreamstime; bouillon © Sebastian Vera/iStockphoto; stopwatch © Kelpfish/Dreamstime; covered pot © Igor Kovalchuk/Shutterstock. Page 8: Cotton swabs © Oreste Gaspari/iStockphoto. Page 9: Mold in petri dish © Guntars Grebezs/iStockphoto. Page 10: Plastic sandwich bag © Nemanja Pesic/iStockphoto; silver spoon © Алексей Брагин/iStockphoto; paper towel © 1MoreCreative/iStockphoto. Page 11: Measuring cup © Blueee/Dreamstime.com; bubbles © Tihis/Dreamstime. Page 12: Garlic press © Anna Chelnokova/Dreamstime; funnel © Vladimir Konjushenko/Dreamstime. Page 13: Full balloon © inxti/Shutterstock; deflated balloon © Alasdair Thomson/iStockphoto; fish sauce © Robert Bremec/iStockphoto; coffee © Barbra Bergfeldt/iStockphoto; notebook © Anna Yu/iStockphoto. Page 14: Stopwatch © Kelpfish/Dreamstime; bowl of ice © Dave White/iStockphoto; shortening on spoon © Fresh Food Images/Photolibrary. Page 15: Hand © Alexander Chernyakov/iStockphoto; duct tape © Keith Webber Jr./iStockphoto. Page 17: Sea lion © Jeffrey Banke/Dreamstime. Page 18: Red cabbage © Win Nondakowit/Dreamstime; microwave © Reflekcija/Dreamstime. Page 19: Blender © Geoffrey Poulad/Dreamstime; smoothie © ma-k/iStockphoto; lemon © dmax-foto/iStockphoto. Page 20: Milk jug © Uyen Le/iStockphoto; vinegar bottle © Sharon Day/iStockphoto; strainer © Petr Malyshev/Dreamstime. Page 21: Glue © Charles Brutlag/Dreamstime; curds © AjFile/Shutterstock. Page 22: Food coloring © Hauntedtoys/Dreamstime. Page 23: Gel on hand © Uppercut Images/Photolibrary; green slime drip © somchaij/Shutterstock; green slime bubbles © Alexander Kuzovlev/iStockphoto. Page 24: Sardine © Hakan Dere/iStockphoto. Page 25: Calendar © Alesandar Jocic/Dreamstime. Page 26: Water faucet © Okea/iStockphoto; garbage can © Skip ODonnell/iStockphoto. Page 27: Mummy © Goran Bogicevic/Dreamstime; along the Nile © Styve Reineck/Shutterstock. Page 28: Chicken bones © Hellem/Dreamstime; jam jar © mm88/iStockphoto. Page 29: Rubber chicken © Nancy Louie/iStockphoto. Page 30: Bowl of flour © Mazzzur/Shutterstock; ball of dough © Cristian Mihai Vela/iStockphoto. Page 31: Helping hands © Сергей Дашкевич/iStockphoto. Page 32: Banana © Steven von Niederhausern/iStockphoto; glass container © James McQuillan/iStockphoto; Page 33: Maggots © Ionescu Bogdan Cristian/iStockphoto; magnifying glass © Baris Simsek/iStockphoto. Page 34: Garlic © Eva Gründemann/Dreamstime; garlic clove © Richardtkeech/Dreamstime; empty glass © rocksunderwater/iStockphoto; rubbing alcohol © Joe Potato Photo/iStockphoto; aluminum foil © Kevin Dyer/iStockphoto. Page 35: Bubbles © Laurent Renault/Dreamstime; bubble wand © Suzannah Skelton/iStockphoto; olfactory senses © Wikimedia Commons. Page 36: Pile of cornflakes © Piyato/Dreamstime; cornflake borders © garloon/Shutterstock. Page 37: Wooden spoon © Stephen Aaron Rees/Shutterstock; magnet © Richard Cote/iStockphoto. Page 38: Food coloring © Johanna Goodyear/Dreamstime. Page 39: Baking sheet © Don Nichols/iStockphoto; flour on cutting board © Don Nichols/iStockphoto. Page 40: Compost © Mona Makela/iStockphoto; duct tape © Dale Hogan/iStockphoto; empty closet © gremlin/iStockphoto. Page 41: Bacillus © Sebastian Kaulitzki/Shutterstock. Page 42: Glass of orange juice: Paul Johnson/iStockphoto; baking soda © Richard Goerg/iStockphoto; toothbrush © Garsya/Shutterstock. Page 43: Toothpaste © Leah-Anne Thompson/Shutterstock; fizzy bubbles © pashabo/Shutterstock; spinach © Renzzo/Dreamstime. Page 45: Leftover container © Anton Atarikov/Dreamstime. Page 46: Peeled green apple © Feng Yu/Shutterstock; apple core © Victor Burnside/iStockphoto. Page 47: Mixing bowl © Tim Grover/Dreamstime. Page 48: Borax box © Dannyphoto80/Dreamstime; glass bowl © Ilya Akinshin/iStockphoto; measuring spoon © Brenda A. Carson/iStockphoto. Page 49: Silly putty © Tyler Freidenrich; polymer molecule © Martin McCarthy/iStockphoto. Page 50: Soap © Robert Red/Shutterstock; plate © Chukov/Shutterstock. Page 51: TV dinner © mikeledray/Shutterstock; marshmallows © Sean Barley/iStockphoto. Page 52: Roll of paper © Christopher Elwell/Shutterstock ; masking tape © M.E. Mulder/Shutterstock; candy pieces © Yordan Rusev/Dreamstime; bottle of cola © Steven Cukrov/Dreamstime. Page 53: Salt shaker © Suzannah Skelton/iStockphoto; fizzy tablet © Pavel Kosek/Shutterstock. Page 54: Jar © HomeStudio/Shutterstock. Page 55: Jar with lid © akiyoko/Shutterstock; bacteria © Sebastian Kaulitzki/Dreamstime. Page 56: Jars © Volodymyr Krasyuk/Shutterstock; chopped garlic © Andy Brown/Dreamstime; dirty socks © isgaby/iStockphoto; broccoli © violetkaipa/Shutterstock; chopped onions © tirc83/iStockphoto; burned toast © Gcpics/Dreamstime. Page 58: Blue fan © Naruemon Bulwan/Dreamstime. Page 59: Girl holding nose © Horst Petzold/Shutterstock; boy with shoe © Jose Manuel Gelpi Diaz/Dreamstime. Page 60: Empty soda bottle © Jckca/Dreamstime; scissors © Skip ODonnell/iStockphoto. Page 61: Sponge © Lasse Kristensen/Dreamstime; soil levels © Eti Swinford/Dreamstime; worm in soil © Ockra/Dreamstime. Page 63: Pink worms in dirt © Kokhanchikov/Shutterstock; compost © Mona Makela/Dreamstime. Page 64: Certificate © Taiga/Shutterstock.

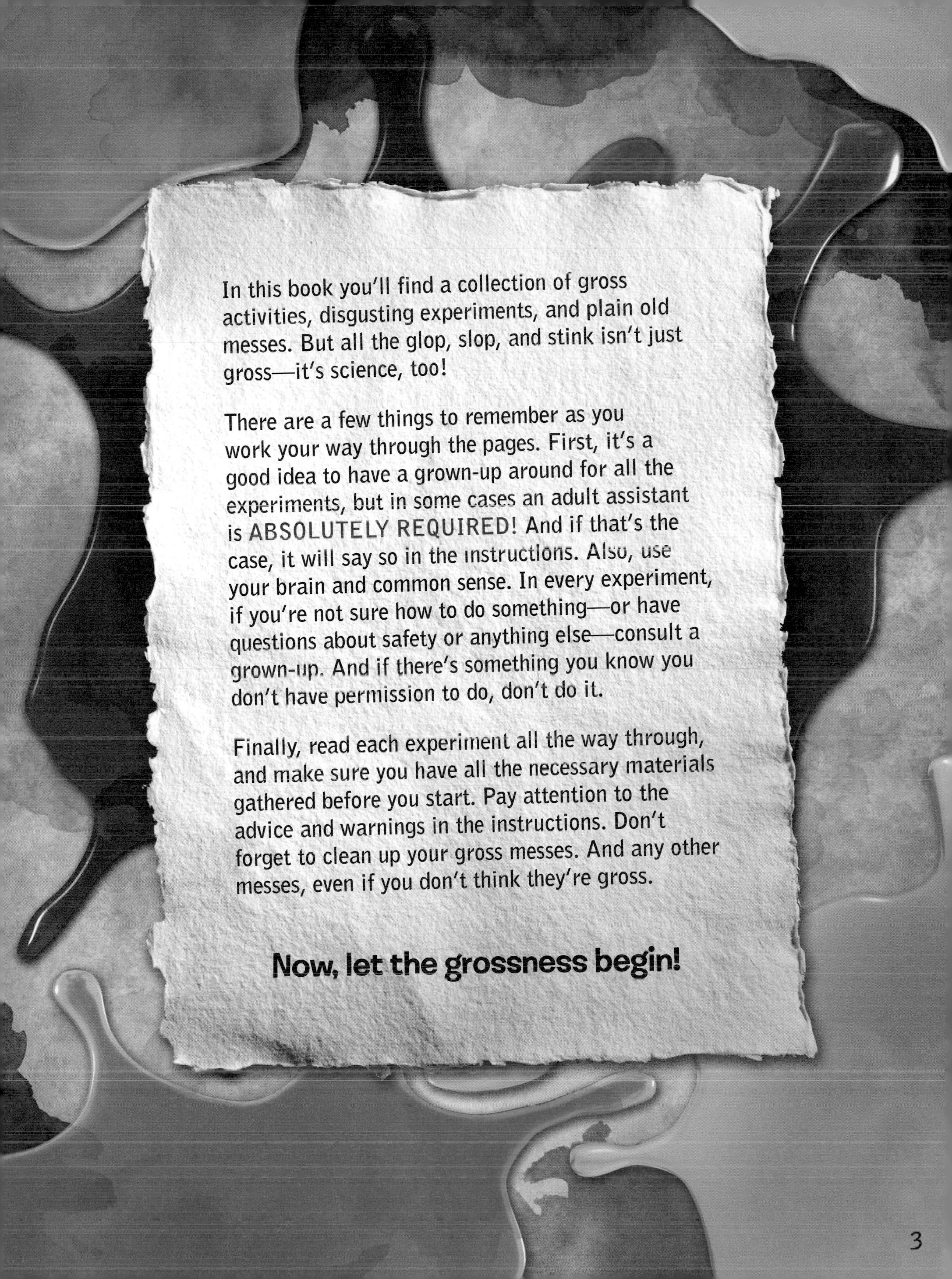

In this book you'll find a collection of gross activities, disgusting experiments, and plain old messes. But all the glop, slop, and stink isn't just gross—it's science, too!

There are a few things to remember as you work your way through the pages. First, it's a good idea to have a grown-up around for all the experiments, but in some cases an adult assistant is ABSOLUTELY REQUIRED! And if that's the case, it will say so in the instructions. Also, use your brain and common sense. In every experiment, if you're not sure how to do something—or have questions about safety or anything else—consult a grown-up. And if there's something you know you don't have permission to do, don't do it.

Finally, read each experiment all the way through, and make sure you have all the necessary materials gathered before you start. Pay attention to the advice and warnings in the instructions. Don't forget to clean up your gross messes. And any other messes, even if you don't think they're gross.

Now, let the grossness begin!

ASPARAGUS? Pee-Ew!

Raise a big stink, just by eating this tasty spear-shaped vegetable!

You'll need:

* A nice, big serving of cooked or raw asparagus (If you don't like asparagus, that will increase the grossness factor!)
* Water (optional)

1 Eat the asparagus. If you want to speed things along, drink a big glass of water, too.

&

2 Amuse yourself however you like until you need to pee.

3 Give in to that call of nature. Go to the bathroom and ... go to the bathroom. While you're at it, take some nice deep breaths through your nose. (Remember, you're doing this for science. And for grossness!) If you're lucky, you'll notice an unusual smell. People have described it as "stinky," "musky," "sulfurous," "fetid," and "like rotting cabbage." What do *you* think?

4 If you don't get gross results, drink some more water, wait a bit, and try again.

There's a chance you still won't get any gross results with this experiment. But that's what makes it an experiment instead of just a trick. Gross scientific studies (yes, scientists study this stuff!) show that some people don't produce smelly urine after eating asparagus. Other people produce it, but can't smell it themselves.

Benjamin Franklin was one of the first scientists to describe the Gross Asparagus Pee Effect. But he didn't call it that.

BEHIND THE GROSS

Scientists still haven't completely solved the mystery of asparagus pee. They agree that the culprit is sulfur, the same element that gives rotten eggs their gross aroma. There are six different sulfur-containing chemicals found in the urine of people who produce smelly asparagus pee—and none in the urine of people who don't. The stink may come from one of these chemicals, or from a combination of them.

SULFUR

Your body may produce the smelly sulfur compounds by breaking down a chemical called asparagusic acid. Young asparagus plants produce this chemical to defend against parasites.

For extra grossness, after you've finished peeing bring a committee of volunteer sniffers into the room. (Warn them about what's going on!) See how many of them can detect the asparagus-urine smell. If no one can smell it, your body probably doesn't produce it.

BACTERIA Farm

Raise a crop of microbes, gathered from your own body!

CAUTION: This experiment uses the stove, so do it only with an adult assistant.

You'll need:

* Adult assistant (REQUIRED—not optional)
* 4 small ceramic or Pyrex (or other heat-safe) bowls (Custard cups work well.)
* Saucepan with lid
* 3 cups (750 ml) water (Distilled or filtered water is best, if you have it.)
* 1 beef bouillon cube
* 1 teaspoon (5 ml) sugar
* Wooden spoon for stirring
* Cotton swabs
* Plastic wrap or foil
* 4 small sheets of paper
* Stove

1 Wash the bowls thoroughly—even if they already look clean!—and let them air dry. After washing them, don't touch the insides of the bowls.

2 Have your adult assistant bring the water to a boil in the saucepan on the stove.

3 Add the bouillon cube and the sugar to the water. This will become the bacteria food. (Even microbes have to eat!)

4 Let the bacteria food boil for 5 minutes. Stir to make sure the bouillon cube is dissolved.

5 Cover the pan and remove it from the heat.

Bacteria Farm continues on the next page.

6 After the bacteria food has cooled a bit, pour it into the bowls. Put the same amount in each bowl.

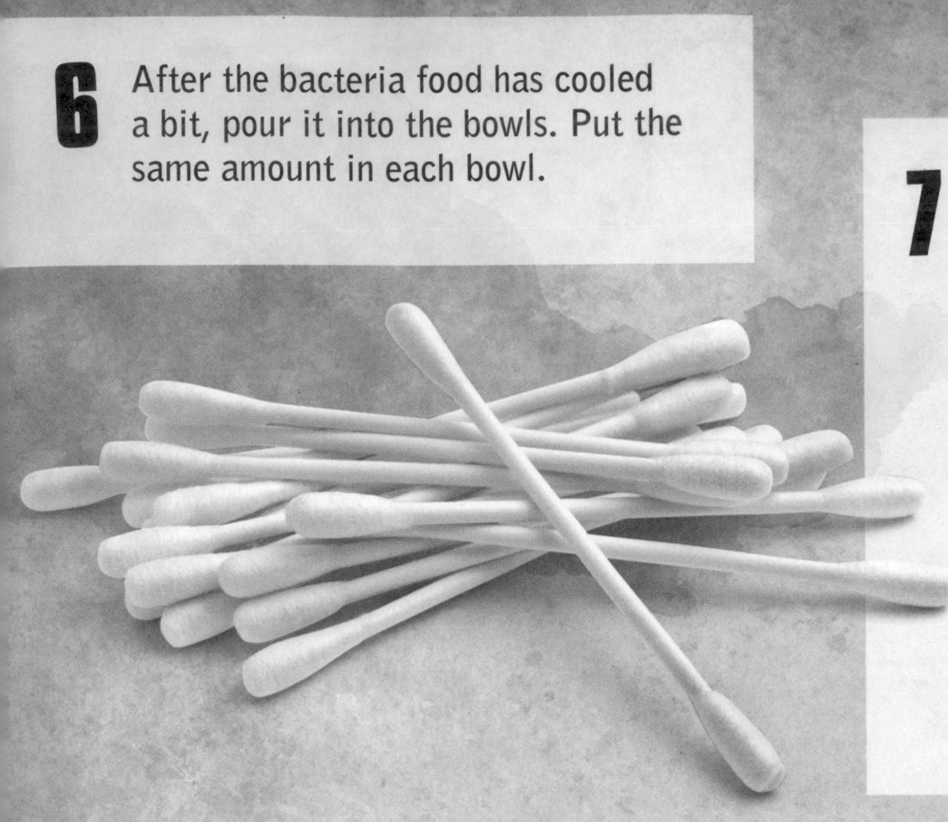

7 It's bacteria-planting time. Take a cotton swab, stick it in your nose (not far—don't hurt yourself!), remove it, and stir the end (the one you stuck in your nose) in one of the bowls. Take a second swab, wipe the end between your toes (right down where things get sweaty), and stir that in the second bowl. Stick your fingers in the third bowl, and leave the fourth bowl alone. (This last bowl is your control, the one you're not adding anything to.) Cover all the bowls with plastic wrap or foil.

8 Find a warm (but not hot) out-of-the-way place to leave your bowls. Lay out the four sheets of paper in a row and put one bowl on each sheet. On the appropriate sheets, write *Nose*, *Toes*, *Fingers*, and *Control*. Just in case, under each label write *Warning: Science experiment. Do not disturb or drink!*

CAUTION:
Don't touch the liquid in the bowls. You don't know whether the bacteria in them are harmful. Once you've examined your bacteria crop, pour the liquid in the toilet and flush it. Wash the bowls thoroughly with soap and water, and then wash your hands.

Leave everything alone for a week. At the end of the week, survey your crop. Check the liquid in the bowls. If it's cloudy, there are bacteria. Clear liquid means no bacteria. Which bowl is the cloudiest? Are there bacteria in the control bowl? If so, what does that tell you? You may get mold or other fungus "weeds" growing in your bacteria farm.

BEHIND THE GROSS

Bacteria are everywhere. There are more of these microbes than any other living thing on the planet. Luckily, only some of them are germs that cause disease. Other bacteria—including microbes in soil, plants, and even your own digestive system—aren't just beneficial, they're essential. Life on Earth couldn't exist without them.

BAKING SODA Popper

It's vinegar and soda POP!

You'll need:

* Sandwich-size zip-sealing plastic bag
* Paper towel
* Scissors
* Measuring spoons
* 2 tablespoons (30 ml) baking soda
* Measuring cup
* ½ cup (120 ml) vinegar
* ¼ cup (60 ml) warm water
* An assistant
* Ruler (optional)

CAUTION: This experiment must be done outdoors.

1 Fill the bag with warm water, zip it closed, and turn it upside down to make sure there aren't any holes. If it leaks, try another bag. If it doesn't, empty out the water, and you're ready to go.

2 Cut the paper towel into a square, about 6 inches (15 cm) on each side.

3 Put the baking soda in the middle of the paper towel. Fold the right and left thirds of the square across the middle, then fold the top and bottom to create a paper-towel envelope with the soda inside.

4 Pour the vinegar into the measuring cup. Add the warm water. Pour the water-vinegar mix into the plastic bag.

5 Take the liquid-filled bag and baking-soda-filled envelope outside to your experiment site.

6 Carefully slip the baking soda envelope into the top of the bag *without letting the paper touch the liquid*. Keep the bag upright! Have your assistant pinch the bag from the outside to hold the envelope in place while you seal up the zipper strips.

7 Tell your assistant to let go. Give the bag a shake, put it on the ground, and stand back. Watch as it begins to swell, then ... *POP!*

BEHIND THE GROSS

Vinegar is a solution of water and acetic (uh-SEED-ick) acid. Baking soda, or sodium bicarbonate, is a base. Whenever an acid and a base mix, there's a chemical reaction. The reaction between the vinegar and the baking soda gives off carbon dioxide (CO_2) gas, creating fizzing, foaming bubbles. Gases take up more space than liquids, so the expanding CO_2 inflates the bag until it bursts.

Balloons of STINK

Where's that awful smell coming from? No one will suspect your ordinary-looking balloon!

You'll need an adult assistant for the first step of this experiment. If you want to keep the rest of it secret, you can dismiss the assistant after that.

CAUTION: Adult assistant required

You'll need:

* Adult assistant (REQUIRED)
* Garlic press or knife
* 1 clove of raw garlic (just one section, not the whole head)
* Large uninflated balloon (latex/rubber, not Mylar)
* ¼ cup (60 ml) water
* Small bowl
* Funnel

1 If you have a garlic press at home, have your adult assistant crush the garlic in the press. If not, have your assistant mince the garlic with a knife. The pieces need to be small enough to fit through the funnel. After that, your adult assistant is no longer needed.

2 Put the crushed/minced garlic into the bowl and add the water. Stir it up.

+ *You can substitute 2 teaspoons (10 ml) of pre-chopped garlic from a jar. Don't use dried garlic or garlic salt. They won't work.*

3 Put the mouth of the funnel into the open neck of the balloon. Try to get it as far in as possible. Keep the funnel upright.

4 Pour the stinky garlic mixture from the bowl through the funnel into the balloon. If any gets stuck, wash it down with a little more water. Don't get any on the outside of the balloon, or you'll ruin the effect.

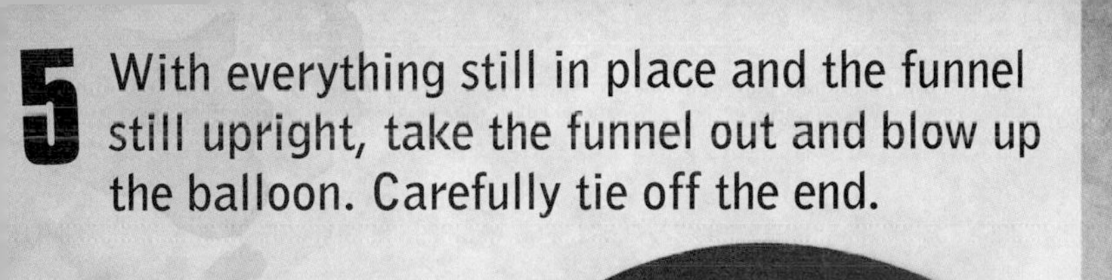

5 With everything still in place and the funnel still upright, take the funnel out and blow up the balloon. Carefully tie off the end.

6 Hide the balloon anywhere you'd like (but not in a drawer or a closet—you want the smell to be able to escape). After about 20 minutes, people will begin to notice the garlic stink. It will get stronger as time goes by.

If the smell isn't moving fast enough for you, you can always stick your nose right on the balloon and take a whiff.

BEHIND THE GROSS

A balloon's rubber skin is actually full of microscopic molecule-sized pores (holes). As the smell molecules spread out from the garlic inside the balloon, some of them pass through the pores—and the stink slowly seeps out into the room.

Air molecules also pass out of and into the balloon through its skin.

Beyond the Gross

Try this same experiment with other smelly substances, such as mashed hard-boiled egg yolk or fish sauce (available where Thai or Vietnamese groceries are sold). For non-gross smells, try ground coffee (you won't need the water) or vanilla extract.

BLUBBERMITT!

Keep warm the whale way—with a thick layer of fat!

If you use a stopwatch, you're going to need an assistant to run it. Your hands will be busy.

You'll need:

* 4 quart-size (0.95-liter) zip-seal plastic bags (the kind you close with your fingers, not with actual plastic zipper sliders)
* 1½ cups (350 ml) vegetable shortening at room temperature
* Duct tape
* Large bowl or small bucket, big and deep enough to put both of your hands in
* Cold water
* Ice cubes
* Clock with second hand or stopwatch
* Ruler (optional)

1 Fill the bowl with cold water. Add some ice cubes and set the bowl aside to get nice and cold.

2 Spoon the shortening into one of the zip-seal bags. Try to get it into the bottom of the bag without getting any on the upper part or the outside.

3 Turn a second bag inside out and slip it inside the first one.

4 Using the zip strips, zip the two bags together to form a double-layered bag with shortening in between. Don't worry if there are small gaps. You'll tape them up in the next step.

5 Roll the open edge of the mitt over to form a one-inch (2.5-cm) "cuff" around the opening. Tape the edge of the cuff all the way around with duct tape.

Blubbermitt! continues on the next page.

6 Squish and move the shortening so you have an even layer of fat all the way around. You've completed your blubbermitt!

7 Make the same kind of mitt out of the other two bags, *but leave out the blubber.*

8 Now it's time for the blubber test. Put the blubbermitt on one hand. Make any fat-squishing adjustments you need in order to get an even layer around your hand. Put the other mitt—the one without blubber in it—on your other hand.

9 Plunge both hands into the ice-cube water. Be careful not to sink them so deep that water gets in over the edges of the mitts. Watch the clock or have your assistant start the stopwatch. When one of your hands gets uncomfortable, take it out of the water. Which hand can stay in longer? Record the times for each hand.

The blubber layer under a large whale's skin can be more than 12 inches (30 cm) thick!

Don't hurt yourself! This isn't an endurance test. You're just trying to see if one hand gets cold faster than the other. Take each hand out as soon as it gets uncomfortable.

BEHIND THE GROSS

Blubber is a thick layer of fat under the skins of whales, seals, and other marine mammals. The fat acts as insulation to keep them warm even in the ice-cold water of the polar oceans. The vegetable fat in your blubbermitt insulates your hand in the same way.

CABBAGE Smoothie

The stink is nice, but the colors are *spectacular*!

CAUTION:
Be safe! Let your adult assistant work the machinery. Knives, blenders, food processors, and stoves can seriously hurt you if used incorrectly.

You'll need:

* Adult assistant (REQUIRED)
* 2–3 cups (480–720 ml) fresh purple or red cabbage (green won't work)
* Measuring cup and measuring spoons
* Spoons
* Water—at least 1½ cups (350 ml)
* Knife
* Blender or food processor
* Microwave oven or stove
* Several small bowls
* 1 tablespoon (15 ml) baking soda
* Lemon or 2 tablespoons (30 ml) lemon juice
* Optional test materials: vinegar and dish soap

1 Have your adult assistant cut the cabbage into small pieces and puree them with water in the blender or food processor. Start with about 1½ cups (350 ml) of water, then add more if needed to make a thick purple (or red) cabbage smoothie.

GROSS TIP: Take a good whiff of the cooked smoothie. Try not to gag.

2 Pour the smoothie into a microwave-safe bowl, and microwave it on the high setting until the mush starts to steam. The amount of time depends on the microwave, so ask your adult assistant for advice.

CAUTION: The bowl will be very hot!

Instead of microwaving, your adult assistant can bring the cabbage mush to a boil in a pan on the stove.

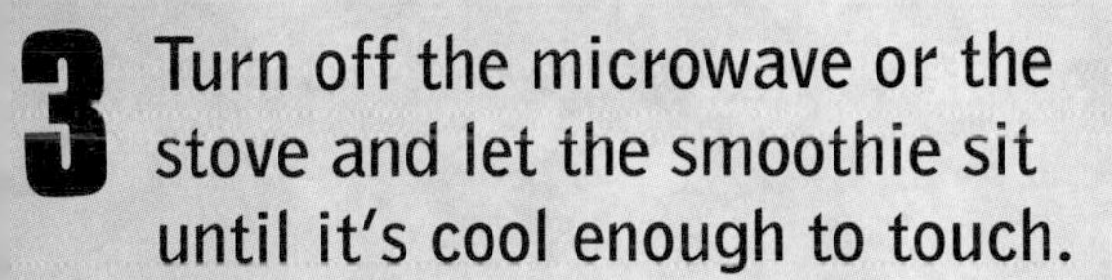

3 Turn off the microwave or the stove and let the smoothie sit until it's cool enough to touch.

4 Pour the smelly mush into three small bowls, or more bowls if you want to do more experiments. Set one bowl of mush aside. That's the control, to show what happens if you don't add anything to the cabbage. Squeeze half a lemon (or pour the lemon juice) into one of the bowls. Stir the juice and smoothie together, and you'll get mush of a different color. Now stir the baking soda into another bowl and see what happens. You can use more lemon juice and baking soda to increase the effects!

5 The gross finale! For the *crème de la blecch*, pour the pink and blue-green smoothies together in a large bowl and give them a quick stir. What color is the fizzing, foaming glop?

CLEANUP:
When you're done, dump the smoothie into the compost or garbage. Don't pour it down the drain, or you may end up with a clogged sink (and an annoyed adult assistant)!

If you have smoothie left over, try the same experiment with vinegar and dish soap. How do the colors compare?

BEHIND THE GROSS

The natural dye in the cabbage changes color when mixed with chemicals called acids and bases. Acids are what give lemon juice and vinegar their sour taste. Baking soda is a base. Acids turn the purple dye pink. Bases turn it blue-green. The stronger the acid or base, the bolder the color change.

CURD Crud

Amaze your friends and gross out your family with a sculpture made from a lump of solid milk!

You'll need:

* Adult assistant (REQUIRED)
* 1½ cups (350 ml) *nonfat* milk
* 4 teaspoons (20 ml) white vinegar
* Microwave-safe bowl
* Microwave oven
* Strainer

1 Put the milk and the vinegar in the microwave-safe bowl and stir them together.

CAUTION: This experiment involves VERY hot liquids and requires an adult assistant.

&

2 Microwave the milk-vinegar mixture for 1 minute and 30 seconds on high.

3 Take the bowl out.

CAUTION: The bowl may be hot. The milk will have separated into liquid and solid parts. Give it a stir to clump the solid parts together.

4 Over the sink, empty the bowl into the strainer and strain away all the liquid. You'll be left with a squishy lump of curd.

When milk separates into liquid with solid lumps and clumps, it has curdled. The lumps are called curds, and the liquid is called whey.

5 When it's cool enough to handle, you can mold the rubbery curd like modeling clay. Sculpt it into whatever shape you'd like—perhaps a curd bird, or a cow from the curd herd, or just an abstract lump of grossness. The curd will harden as it cools. Put your milk sculpture in the refrigerator to make it extra-hard. (And extra-gross.)

Keep your curd sculpture in mind the next time you eat a piece of cheese.

BEHIND THE GROSS

Milk is a mixture of water, fat, and solid parts called milk solids, made up of protein and carbohydrate. Fresh out of the cow, the milk is 88 percent water, 5 percent fat, and 7 percent milk solids. Virtually all of the fat is taken out of nonfat milk, leaving just the water and milk solids.

Adding vinegar (an acid) causes the milk to curdle, separating the curds from the whey. The heat from the microwave makes this chemical reaction happen faster.

The rubbery texture of your curd lump comes from a protein called casein (KAY-seen). This milk protein was used to make an early form of plastic. It is also sometimes an ingredient in white glue.

If your curd was too mushy, try the experiment again. But this time, microwave the mixture for 1 minute and 45 seconds.

CAUTION:
The bowl might be very hot.

Fake SNOT

It's gooey! It's snotty! It's fake!

You'll need:

* Adult assistant (REQUIRED—whether you're using the microwave or the stove)
* Pyrex (heat-safe glass) measuring cup
* ½ cup (120 ml) water
* 3 packs unflavored gelatin (That's 3 individual packets, *not whole boxes!*)
* Green and/or yellow food coloring (optional)
* ½ cup (120 ml) light corn syrup
* Wooden spoon for stirring
* Microwave oven or stove

1 Put the water in the Pyrex measuring cup. Heat it in the microwave on high just until it reaches the boiling point. (That's when it starts to steam.) The amount of time required will depend on your microwave.

CAUTION: This experiment involves boiling water, so it requires an adult assistant. Also, the glass cup can get VERY hot.

Instead of using a microwave, you can have your adult assistant heat the water in a pan on the stove. When it reaches the boiling point, pour it back into the Pyrex measuring cup.

2 Pour all three packs of gelatin into the water. For extra-gross snot, add a couple of drops of green and/or yellow food coloring. Stir with the spoon until all the gelatin has dissolved. Set the cup aside to cool for 60 seconds.

3 After 60 seconds, pour the corn syrup into the mixture. Give it a stir. Lift the spoon and watch the long, stringy strands of snot drip oozingly back into the cup.

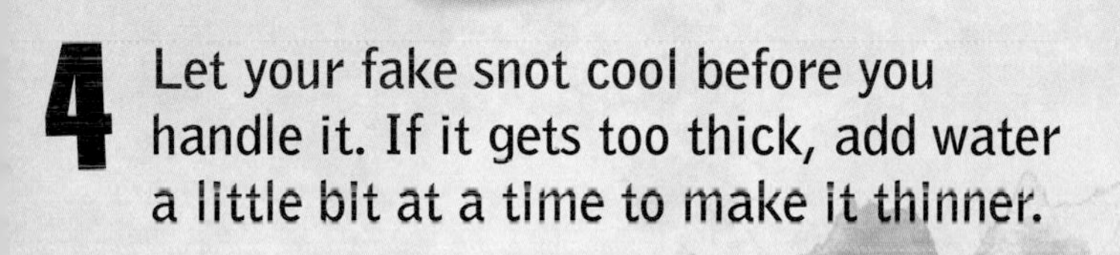

4 Let your fake snot cool before you handle it. If it gets too thick, add water a little bit at a time to make it thinner.

After the fake snot has cooled, stick your hand in it. Feels like the real thing, doesn't it? Pretend to sneeze, then hold up your gooey hand to gross out your friends and family. Then put the gross icing on the disgusting cake by licking it!

Adding water to your cup of snot is like drinking lots of water if your nose is stuffed solid with gooey mucus when you have a cold. More water in your body puts more water in the snot, making it thinner.

If you want thicker snot next time, use a little less water or more gelatin. You can safely lick this fake snot because it's made of food ingredients. (We're not saying it will taste good, but it's better than the real thing!) Do not try tasting other snot recipes you may have seen! Many of them use glue and borax, *which you should not eat.*

BEHIND THE GROSS

Like the other slimy mixtures in this book, snot (real or fake) is a polymer, a chemical made of linked, chainlike molecules. If you've ever been outside in the cold and used your hand to wipe your nose (c'mon, we've all been there!), you know the mucus from your nose is normally clear. When you're sick and not just cold, your snot can be green, because of chemicals produced by your immune system.

FISH Mummy

There's no de-Nile that a mummy is a piece of classic grossness!

If you don't catch fish yourself or have a fresh fish market nearby, a fish from the grocery store is fine. The smaller the fish, the quicker—and less expensive!—the mummy. Trout is good, but smelt is even better. You'll get a grosser mummy if the fish still has its head attached. You can even use a frozen fish (whole—a fillet makes a boring mummy), but make sure to thaw it first.

You'll need:

* Adult assistant (very helpful for this one)
* A small whole fish, cleaned (gutted) and scaled
* Large box of baking soda (Depending on the size of your fish, you may need two large boxes.)
* Large mixing bowl
* 1-gallon (3.785-liter) heavyweight zip-seal bag
* Paper towels

1 Rinse the fish inside and out, then pat it dry with paper towels, also inside and out.

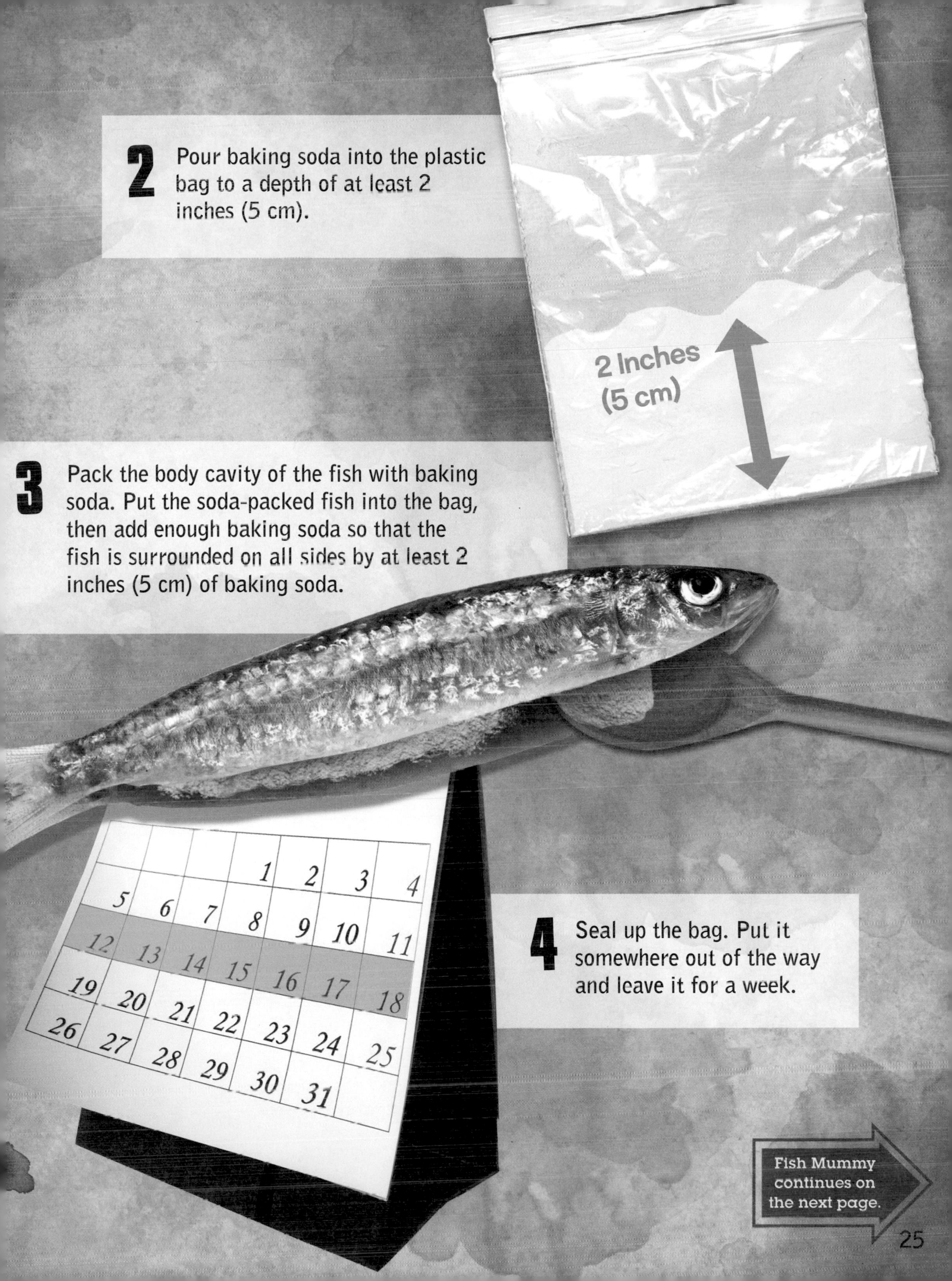

2 Pour baking soda into the plastic bag to a depth of at least 2 inches (5 cm).

3 Pack the body cavity of the fish with baking soda. Put the soda-packed fish into the bag, then add enough baking soda so that the fish is surrounded on all sides by at least 2 inches (5 cm) of baking soda.

4 Seal up the bag. Put it somewhere out of the way and leave it for a week.

Fish Mummy continues on the next page.

5 After a week, open the bag and take the fish out. Prepare yourself for any gross smells you might encounter. Brush off the baking soda. Do you notice any changes?

6 Throw away all the baking soda in the bag.

7 Clean out and throw away the soda from inside the fish's body cavity and any soda still stuck to the outside. (Brush off the soda. *Don't use water*, or you'll wreck the mummy!) Repack the fish with fresh baking soda, inside and out. Seal up the bag and leave it for another week.

8 At the end of the second week, you should have a dry, shriveled, gross-looking fish mummy. If it's not quite mummified, change the baking soda again and give it another few days.

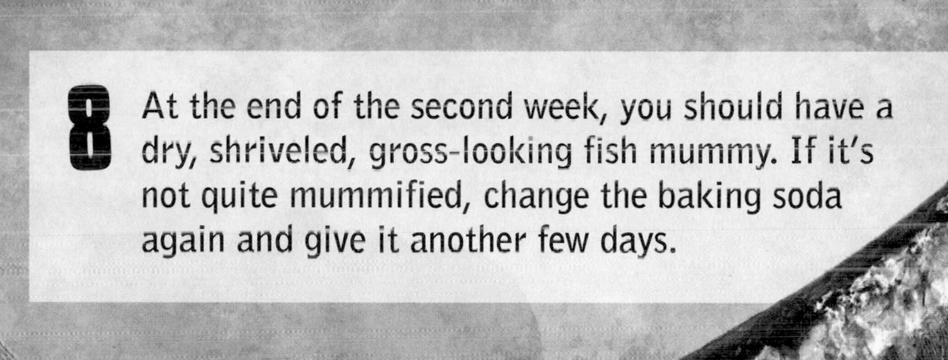

BEHIND THE GROSS

The baking soda mummified the fish by dehydrating it, or drawing all the water out of its body. If you touch a tiny bit of baking soda to your tongue (fresh, not from the mummy), you'll notice that it's salty. Salts, like baking soda, act as dehydrators, drawing out and absorbing water molecules. That's why you get thirsty when you eat salty foods.

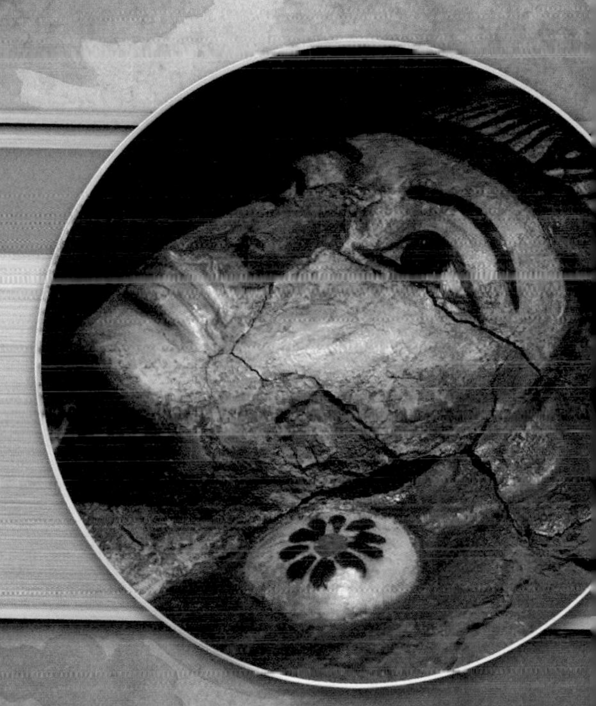

Ancient grossness

The ancient Egyptians dehydrated their mummies with a salt called natron, found on the banks of the Nile River. Natron consists mostly of sodium carbonate (washing soda) with sodium bicarbonate (baking soda) and small amounts of other salts.

Flexible BONE

Ordinary vinegar makes a hard chicken bone go all wobbly!

You'll need:

* Bone from a chicken leg or thigh (Save one the next time you have chicken for dinner.)
* Jar with lid
* White vinegar (enough to fill the jar several times)

1 Clean all the leftover meat, skin, blood vessels, and other gross material off the bone. (Otherwise, this will turn into a very stinky experiment, but not in an interesting way.) Rinse the cleaned bone under running water.

2 Put the bone in the jar. Fill the jar with vinegar. Make sure it covers the bone completely.

The jar should be big enough for the bone to fit in, but not so big that you waste a lot of vinegar.

3 Close the jar and leave it in an out-of-the-way place for three days.

Take a peek at the bone from time to time. It should be covered with tiny bubbles.

4 After three days, pour out the vinegar, remove the bone from the jar, and rinse it off. Test the bone for flexibility. (It probably won't be very flexible yet.) Put the bone back in the jar, cover it with fresh vinegar, close the jar, and leave it for another three days.

5 Keep testing the bone and changing the vinegar every three days, until the bone becomes flexible and rubbery.

Contrary to popular belief, the rubber chickens used in comedy routines don't have rubber bones. They're filled with air. Your real rubber chicken bone is cooler and way, *way* grosser.

Your own bones need calcium to get the minerals that make them strong. That's why it's important for you to have enough calcium in your diet.

BEHIND THE GROSS

The hard, rigid part of bone is made of minerals, mostly calcium phosphate and calcium carbonate. The minerals make up about 70 percent of the bone material. The other 30 percent is made of fibers of a material called collagen, plus blood vessels, nerves, and other tissue. Chemical reactions between acetic acid in the vinegar and the minerals in the bone break down the minerals. Some of their components, like the calcium atoms and phosphate molecules, dissolve into the liquid. One of the reactions also gives off carbon dioxide gas, which turn up as the bubbles on the bone. Eventually, all the minerals are gone, leaving only the flexible, rubbery stuff.

Glutinous DOUGH BALL

Turn ordinary flour into a gluey, stretchy glob!

You'll need:

* 1-2 cups (240–480 ml) 100 percent whole wheat flour
* ¾ cup (180 ml) water
* Mixing bowl
* Plate
* Sink
* Other types of flour (optional)

1 Mix the water and 1 cup (240 ml) of flour together in a mixing bowl.

2 Stick your hands in and start mixing. Add more flour until the mixture is firm enough to form a ball of dough. Take the ball out of the bowl and knead it in your hands until it has an even, slightly rubbery texture all the way through.

3 Get to know your dough ball. Roll it around in your hands. Pinch and rub it between your fingers to feel the texture. Squish and stretch it to see how it behaves.

If your dough is too thin or runny, add more flour.

4 Put the dough on a plate and let it rest for 15 minutes.

5 Run a gentle stream of warm water in the sink. Cup your hands around your dough ball and hold it under the stream. Gently squeeze and roll the ball in your hands as the water runs over it. The water running off the ball will become cloudy with starch. Keep squeezing and rolling the dough ball until the water running over it is clear.

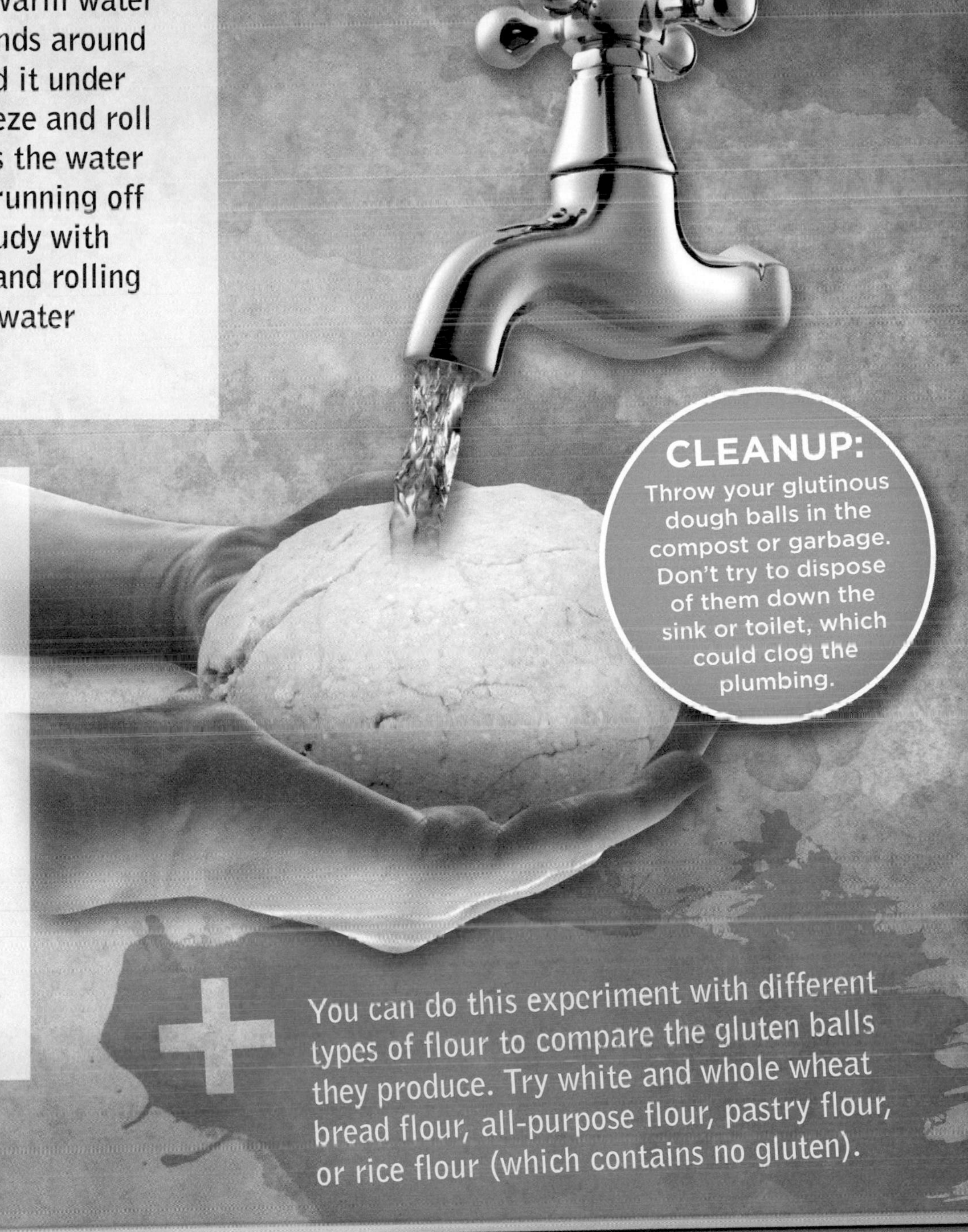

CLEANUP: Throw your glutinous dough balls in the compost or garbage. Don't try to dispose of them down the sink or toilet, which could clog the plumbing.

6 You're now holding a ball made of almost nothing but gluten, along with some fiber. Squish and stretch the glutinous dough ball. Feel the texture. How does it compare with the dough ball before you rinsed the starch out? More important, does it feel more or less gross?

You can do this experiment with different types of flour to compare the gluten balls they produce. Try white and whole wheat bread flour, all-purpose flour, pastry flour, or rice flour (which contains no gluten).

BEHIND THE GROSS

The word *gluten* comes from the Latin word for glue, and that's what gluten is. It's the protein "glue" that holds the dough together in bread, noodles, and other foods made from wheat. When you add water to dry flour and start mixing, the gluten forms long strands of protein. The more you knead the dough, the more the strands of gluten stretch—and the more stretchy the dough becomes. Different foods made with flour need different amounts of gluten. Bread and noodles need stretchy, firm dough, so the flour for making them has the most gluten. Foods like cakes and pastries need to be more delicate and crumbly, so cake and pastry flours have less gluten.

MAGGOT Roundup

Watch adorably gross fruit fly maggots as they hatch and grow!

CAUTION:
This project is best done outdoors in warm weather. Don't do it indoors, or you could end up with a fruit-fly infestation in your house!

You'll need:

* Large jar
* Nylon stocking or leg cut from a pair of pantyhose (or a piece of other "breathable" fabric)
* Rubber band
* Banana
* Magnifying glass (optional)

1 Peel the banana and put it in the jar. Set the jar outside in the shade (not in the sun).

2 Leave the jar outside for a few days. Check it often to look for small fruit flies. When there are a good number of flies in the jar, trap them inside by putting the stocking over it. Put the rubber band around the rim to hold the mesh in place.

3 Keep the flies in the jar for a few days to give them time to lay eggs. Then, take off the stocking and let the flies out. Put the stocking back on, to keep other insects out.

As the comedian Groucho Marx once said, "Time flies like an arrow. Fruit flies like a banana."

4 Sit back and wait for the maggots! Actually, it will take a few days for them to hatch. They're small, so a magnifying glass may help. The maggots look like tiny worms. They'll crawl all over the banana, burrowing into it as they eat. Eventually, the maggots will form pupae, which look like little grains of rice. A couple weeks after first hatching, adult flies will emerge from the pupae.

Gross as they are, maggots are an important part of the environment. They help break down dead and decaying material, which then returns to the soil and nourishes new living things.

When they're grown, let your fruit flies go. Dump any leftover rotten banana in the garbage or compost (outdoors, not in the house!), rinse out the jar, and recycle it.

BEHIND THE GROSS

Larva is the stage of an insect's life right after it hatches from the egg. (The plural of *larva* is *larvae*.) Butterfly larvae are called caterpillars, which sounds nice. Fly larvae are called maggots, which sounds gross. And most maggots *are* pretty gross! They hatch from the eggs laid by flies in rotting meat, dead animals, poop, garbage, and lots of other disgusting, decaying materials. Worse yet, as soon as the maggots hatch, they start eating the gross stuff they were born in. Compared to others, fruit fly maggots are downright cute. Sure, the fruit they eat is rotten, but it smells a lot better than a dead skunk.

Malodorous BUBBLES

They float gently through the air. But when they pop—look out!

You'll need:

* Adult assistant (REQUIRED)
* 1 large clove of garlic
* Garlic press or chopping knife (for use by your adult assistant!)
* Cup
* 1 teaspoon (5 ml) rubbing alcohol
* Foil or plastic wrap
* 1 tablespoon (15 ml) liquid dish soap (or ⅓ cup [80 ml] premixed bubble solution)
* 5 tablespoons (75 ml) water
* Spoon
* Bubble-blowing wand (from a toy bubble set)
* Strong-smelling stuff like ground coffee, Parmesan cheese, or vanilla extract (optional)

1 With the help of your adult assistant, squeeze the garlic through the garlic press into the cup. If you don't have a garlic press, have your assistant mince the garlic with a knife, then put the minced garlic in the cup.

CAUTION: This experiment requires an adult assistant.

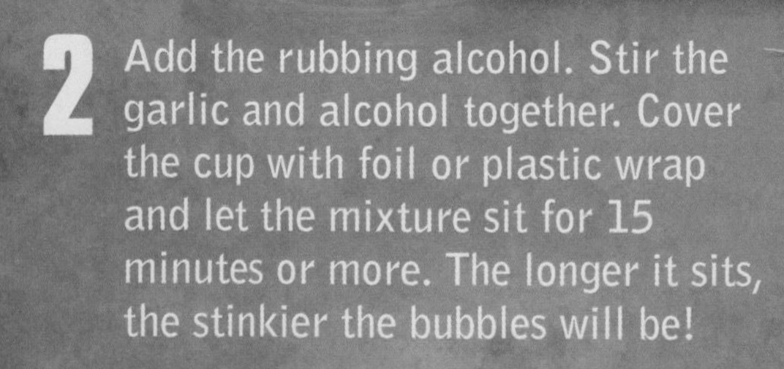

2 Add the rubbing alcohol. Stir the garlic and alcohol together. Cover the cup with foil or plastic wrap and let the mixture sit for 15 minutes or more. The longer it sits, the stinkier the bubbles will be!

3 Add the dish soap to the cup, then add the water. Stir the mixture gently with a spoon. You want to mix well, *but not make suds.*

You can use premixed toy bubble solution instead of dish soap: Put in 1/3 cup (80 ml) of the solution, and don't add any water.

Non-ultra concentrated **dish soap (such as Dawn® or Joy®) is best for this experiment. Don't use antibacterial soap.**

4 Find an unsuspecting victim (or try it on yourself). Dip the bubble wand in the cup and blow some bubbles into the air. Ask your victim to pop them. Smell anything?

For the full stink effect, pop the bubbles with your nose!

BEHIND THE GROSS

Your sense of smell is all about molecules. The nasal passages behind your nose are lined with special smell-detecting nerve cells, covered by a layer of runny mucus. When you breathe in, scent molecules in the air go up your nose and get trapped in the mucus layer. The smell detecting cells detect the molecules and send information to your brain.

When you blow a garlic bubble, the garlic scent molecules are trapped in the bubble solution, so you can't smell them. When the bubble pops—presto stinko!—the molecules spread out into the air.

Try the stink bubble solution with other strong-smelling substances, such as 1 teaspoon (5 ml) of ground coffee or grated Parmesan cheese. If you want better-smelling bubbles, a quarter teaspoon of vanilla extract will do the trick. (When using vanilla, leave out the rubbing alcohol.)

Metal BREAKFAST

Go fishing for iron in ordinary breakfast cereal!

If you don't have any iron-fortified cereal around the house, this is the perfect excuse to get your parents to buy that cereal they don't usually let you have.

You'll need:

* Measuring cup
* ½ cup (120 ml) of any breakfast cereal fortified with iron
* 1-quart or larger zip-seal plastic bag
* Glass or plastic mixing bowl (not metal!)
* 1 cup (240 ml) water
* Magnet (Clean off any stray bits of stuff that are stuck to it.)
* Wooden or plastic mixing spoon (again, not metal)

1 Pour the cereal into the plastic bag. Zip it closed.

ABOUT THE CEREAL

Check the nutrition label on the box to make sure your cereal is fortified with iron. It will be listed with the vitamins and minerals. The more iron, the better. Some cereals have as much as 90 percent of the daily iron requirement in each serving.

2 Crunch up the cereal inside the bag. When it's good and smashed, open the bag and pour the crunched-up cereal into the mixing bowl.

3 Add the water to the bowl. Drop in the magnet and start stirring. Stir the magnet for at least five minutes. Ten is even better. If the mixture isn't runny enough to stir, add more water.

ABOUT THE MAGNET

Any small (but not tiny) or medium-size magnet works fine, including refrigerator magnets. Just remember that you're going to be stirring it up in a bowl of mushy cereal and water, so don't use a magnet that has cardboard or paper attached.

4 Reach into the bowl (Ick!) and fish out the magnet. Rinse the cereal goo off the magnet with VERY gently running water.

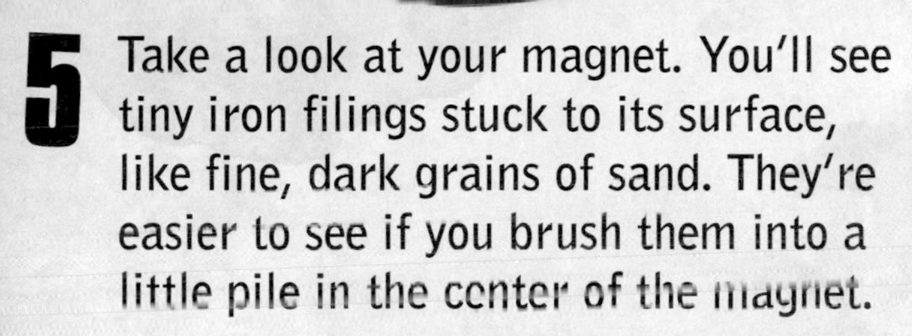

5 Take a look at your magnet. You'll see tiny iron filings stuck to its surface, like fine, dark grains of sand. They're easier to see if you brush them into a little pile in the center of the magnet.

BEHIND THE GROSS

Who knew you were munching metal with your breakfast? Most cold cereals have extra, added vitamins and minerals to help you get the amount your body needs every day. One of those minerals is iron, in the form of tiny grains of pure metal. The metal reacts with acid in your stomach to create iron ions (electrically charged particles). Your small intestine absorbs the iron ions into your bloodstream.

Blood and Iron

Iron is an important building block for the molecules of the protein called hemoglobin (HEE-mo-glow-bin). That's the chemical in your red blood cells that carries oxygen. The iron in hemoglobin is also what gives blood its red color.

Miracle GLOP

Liquid? Solid? Gross!

You'll need:

* Large mixing bowl
* ½ cup (120 ml) water
* 1-lb. (.45-kg) box cornstarch (You won't use it all, but you want to be sure you have enough.)
* Measuring cup
* Spoon or stick for stirring
* Food coloring (optional)
* Newspaper (optional)

1 Pour the water into the mixing bowl.

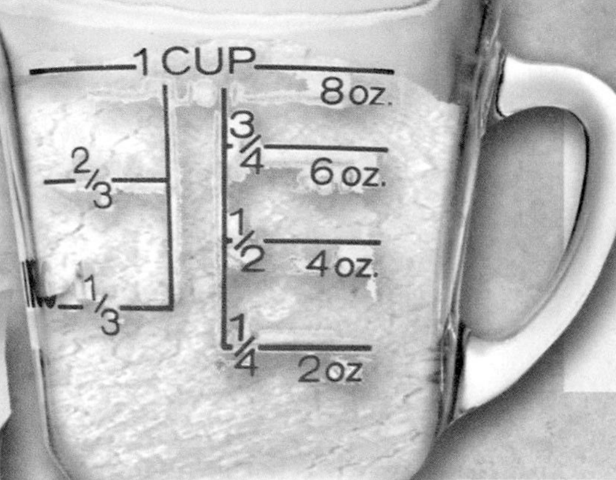

2 Measure out 1 level cup (240 ml) of cornstarch.

For extra grossness, add two drops each of red, yellow, and blue food coloring. You won't just get glop, you'll get horrible *brown* glop.

3 Start sprinkling the cornstarch into the water a little at a time while stirring the mixture. Keep sprinkling and stirring until you've added the whole cup. Eventually, you'll have to start using your fingers instead of the spoon. You want the mixture to be about as thick as a thick milkshake. If it's too powdery, add more water. If it's too runny, add more cornstarch.

+ If you want more or less glop, change the amounts of the ingredients you use. You always want twice as much cornstarch as water.

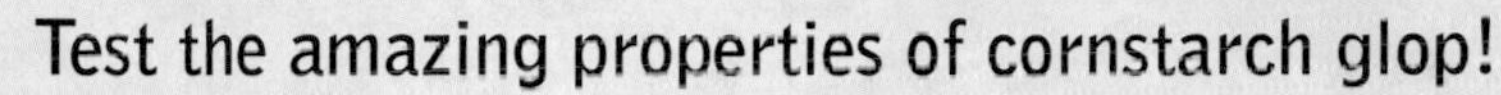

You'll notice that the glop gets harder to stir as it thickens, eventually stopping the spoon dead in its tracks. Like magic, if you stir more slowly everything works fine.

4 Test the amazing properties of cornstarch glop!

* Pinch it between your fingers. What do you notice?
* Grab a fistful. It feels solid when you squeeze, but goes runny as soon as your hand relaxes.
* Tap the glop in the bowl with your fingers. It feels solid and rubbery. But push gently and your fingers sink right in.
* Pour some glop onto a cookie sheet. It's probably best to spread out some sheets of newspaper under the cookie sheet first, just in case. Slap your hand down on the runny goo. What happens? Where's the splatter? (If it does splatter, it's too runny. Add a little more cornstarch to the glop you have left.)

BEHIND THE GROSS

The cornstarch-and-water mixture is called a colloid (CAL-oyd). It consists of tiny cornstarch particles suspended in water. Cornstarch is a polymer, meaning it's made of long, chainlike molecules. When you press or squeeze the glop hard and fast, the molecules don't have time to slip around one another. They get tangled up, and the glop acts like a solid. If you press gently, the cornstarch particles slip around one another, and the glop acts like a liquid.

CLEANUP: DO NOT pour your cornstarch glop down the drain or flush it down the toilet! It will clog the pipes. When it's time to get rid of it, toss the glop in the compost or the garbage.

GLOP STORAGE

If you want to save your glop for further experiments, you can store it in a zip-seal plastic bag. It will eventually dry out, so you may have to add more water.

MOLD Museum

Create a repulsive display with nothing but table scraps.

This project is not for the impatient or the faint of heart. It takes time (and a strong stomach), but the payoff is worth it.

You'll need:

* Jar with a lid
* Duct tape
* Scraps of food, like old fruit, bread crusts, and potato peelings

1 Drop food scraps into the jar. Fill it up about halfway.

You don't need to worry about cleaning the jar before you start. The dirtier, the better!

2 Screw the lid onto the jar tightly.

3 Seal the lid with duct tape.

4 Set the jar in a warm, dark, out-of-the-way place. (The warmth and darkness encourage the growth of bacteria and mold. The quiet location helps make sure no one knocks the jar onto the floor.)

5 Wait. Check the jar in a couple days. Check it again in a week. If you're lucky, you'll see a colorful, ever-changing showcase of wild bacteria and mold.

CAUTION: After sealing the jar, do NOT open it or touch anything inside it. The stuff could make you really **sick.**

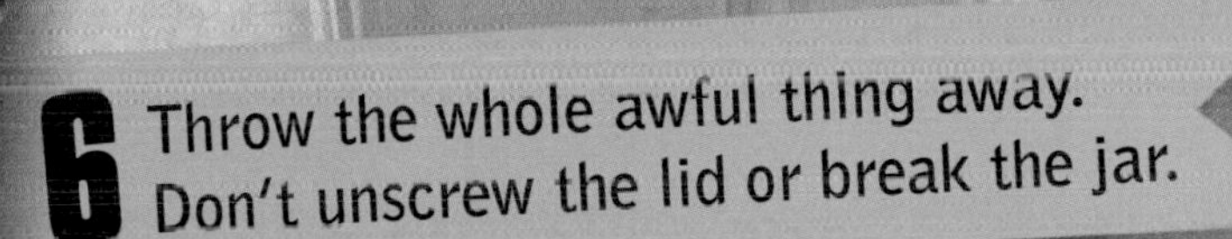

6 Throw the whole awful thing away. Don't unscrew the lid or break the jar.

+ Sketch or photograph the jar every day. Can you discover when the growth really takes off? How long does it take to slow down?

BEHIND THE GROSS

What happened to turn those perfectly respectable scraps into an exhibit with an Ick Factor of 10? Bacteria and mold, that's what happened. The air around us is filled with all kinds of simple organisms, such as bacteria and mold. If they settle on something they can use as a food source, like the table scraps in the jar, they eat and multiply until they form clumps and colonies big enough for us to see.

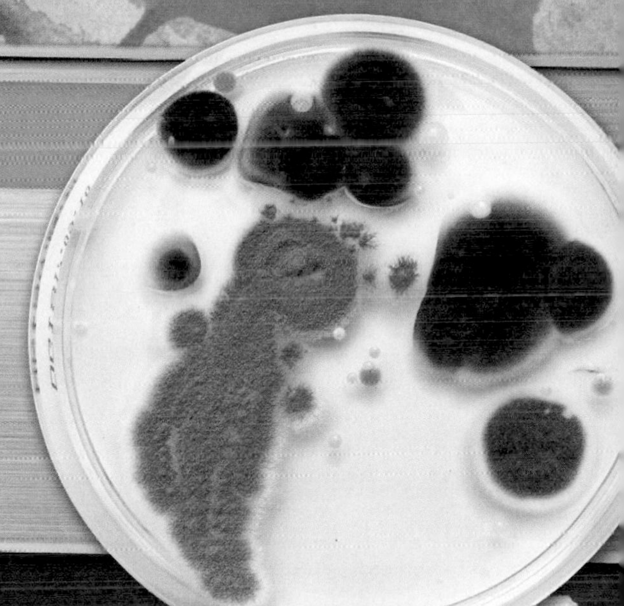

Photograph of bacilli often found in soil

Bacteria and Mold

Bacteria (the singular is *bacterium*) are single-celled organisms that live just about everywhere: in the air, in the ground, and even in our bodies. They come in three main shapes, each with a special scientific name: rods (called bacilli), spirals (spirilla), and balls (cocci).

Molds are a different kind of organism from bacteria. Along with mushrooms and mildew, they belong to a different kingdom of living things: the fungi. Molds aren't single-celled.

Orange YUCK

Ordinary toothpaste transforms delicious orange juice into a mouthful of disgustingness!

Don't worry—you don't have to eat or drink the toothpaste. That's good, because swallowing toothpaste is not just gross—it's bad for you.

You'll need:

* Glass of orange juice
* Baking soda
* Toothbrush
* Sink and water
* Toothpaste containing sodium lauryl sulfate

Check the ingredients of your regular toothpaste to make sure it contains sodium lauryl sulfate. Most toothpastes do, but some (such as Tom's of Maine®) don't.

1 Take a sip of the orange juice. Isn't it delicious?

2 Rinse your mouth out with water. Now, put a little baking soda in your hand, wet your toothbrush, dip the bristles in the baking soda, and then brush your teeth. The taste is pretty high on the grossness scale already!

IMPORTANT:

Be very gentle with the toothbrushing. Baking soda was used as toothpaste in the old days, and some people still brush with it. But it is very abrasive (scratchy) and could harm your teeth if you use it by itself every day.

3 Give your mouth and the toothbrush a good rinse.

4 Take another drink of orange juice. Does it taste different? If so, does it taste gross?

5 Now, brush your teeth with the toothpaste. Brush for at least a minute. Once again, rinse your mouth and your toothbrush.

The baking soda is the control test, to make sure it's the toothpaste, and not the brushing, that gets gross results.

6 Take another drink of orange juice. If you're lucky (in the gross department, that is) your taste buds will tell you, "Yuck!"

BEHIND THE GROSS

Scientists aren't completely certain what's going on here because the sense of taste is a very complicated thing. But they're pretty sure the bitter taste is caused by the sodium lauryl sulfate. This harmless, soaplike chemical gives the foamy frothiness to toothpaste, shampoo, and other products. It also breaks up some oil-like materials called phospholipids (FOSS-foe-LIP-idz) that are typically found on your tongue.

Orange juice is sweet and bitter at the same time, but typically the sweetness makes up for the bitterness. When the phospholipids are removed, your taste buds become much more sensitive to bitterness—and the gross taste overpowers the sweetness.

Spinach

Gross-taste genetics

Back in the 1930s, scientists discovered that two chemicals, called PTC and PROP, caused a gross, bitter taste on the tongues of some people and not others. The difference is caused by variations in a single gene in people's bodies. PTC and PROP aren't found naturally, but the ability to taste them also makes some foods like raw spinach taste gross and bitter to some people.

Rubber EGG

Things get really disgusting when you peel a raw egg!

* Raw egg
* 2–3 cups (480–720 ml) of white vinegar (You might need more.)
* Small mixing bowl (or plastic leftover container with a lid) big enough to hold the egg with extra room on top (If you're using a mixing bowl, you can cover it with plastic wrap or a small plate.)

1 Put the egg in the bowl (or the plastic container). Pour in enough vinegar to cover the whole egg, then add enough extra to raise the vinegar level another inch (2.5 cm).

Take a look at your egg after it's been in the vinegar for an hour or two. It will be covered with tiny bubbles.

2 Cover the bowl and put it in the refrigerator. Find something else to do for 24 hours. You might want to put a note on the lid, so no one tries to eat your egg.

DO NOT EAT!

3 After 24 hours, take the bowl to the sink. Carefully take the egg out and pour the vinegar down the drain. Put the egg back in the bowl.

4 Run some water and rinse the vinegar off your hands.

5 Pour fresh vinegar into the bowl to cover the egg as before. Cover the bowl and put it back in the refrigerator.

6 After another 24 hours, take out the bowl. The egg's shell should be gone. Carefully take out the egg and pour the vinegar down the drain.

7 Rinse off the egg with running water. If there is any shell left, rub it VERY gently with your fingers under the running water, and it should rinse off.

Take a look at your rubbery, shell-less egg. Roll it around in your hand (but don't drop it). Squeeze it (gently, or things will get grosser than you probably want them to). What do you notice about the size?

BEHIND THE GROSS

The secret of the disappearing eggshell is a chemical reaction. Eggshells are made of a base called calcium carbonate. Vinegar is 5 percent acetic acid. (The other 95 percent is water.) The base and acid react with each other to form carbon dioxide—the bubbles you saw on the outside of the egg—and calcium acetate, which dissolves in the water. That leaves only the rubbery inner membrane to hold the egg together.

THE GROSS FINALE

Here's your chance to bounce an egg! It's best to try this in the sink. Drop the egg from an inch or two (2.5–5 cm) above the surface, and it will bounce. For maximum grossness, see how high you can go before it splats. Don't forget to clean up!

The movement of water through the membrane is called osmosis (ahs-MO-siss).

Ballooning up

The egg's membrane lets some molecules, like water, pass through. The egg white inside is about 90 percent water, while the vinegar on the outside is 95 percent water. Water moves through the membrane to equalize the percentage, and the shell-less egg swells up like a water balloon.

Shrunken HEADS

Fake heads, real shrinking!

CAUTION: This experiment involves sharp kitchen tools, so an adult assistant is required.

You'll need:

* Adult assistant (REQUIRED)
* Apple (use more than one at a time if you like)
* Whole cloves (optional)
* 4 cups (1 liter) water
* 2 tablespoons (30 ml) salt
* Large mixing bowl
* Spoon for stirring
* Vegetable peeler
* Small knife or sculpting tool for carving
* Baking soda
* Plate
* Apple corer (optional)
* Lemon juice or lemon (optional)

1 Peel the apple with the vegetable peeler. Leave the stem and a bit of peel on the top for "hair."

CAREFUL: Have your assistant headshrinker help you.

For added grossness you can remove the brains—er, the core—with an apple corer. But it's not necessary.

2 Use the knife or the sculpting tool to carve a face into the apple. Big noses and deep-set eye sockets work really well. If you want, you can stick a couple of cloves into the sockets for eyes. You can eat the pieces of apple you carved away.

3 Pour the water into the bowl. Add the salt and stir until it dissolves.

4 Put the carved apple in the bowl of saltwater and soak it for at least 15 minutes. If you live in a damp climate, soak it longer—up to an hour in really humid places. Turn the head from time to time to make sure it gets wet all over.

If you don't want your shrunken head to turn brown, you can squeeze some lemon juice into the water. Of course, that would make it less gross.

5 Sprinkle a layer of baking soda on the plate. When the head has finished soaking, shake off the excess saltwater and place it on the plate (not face down!). Put the whole thing in a warm, dry place. Don't leave the head in the sun or in a damp place, or it will rot instead of shrinking.

6 Be patient. It may take as long as two weeks for your apple head to shrink and shrivel fully. When it's ready, display your shrunken head on your trophy shelf of grossness—or anywhere else you like.

BEHIND THE GROSS

The salt draws water out of the apple, helping it to dry more quickly without rotting or getting moldy.

Slimy PUTTY

Stiffened slime stretches, bounces, and sags!

You'll need:

* 1 tablespoon (15 ml) borax laundry booster (found in the detergent section of the grocery store)
* 1 tablespoon (15 ml) white glue (such as Elmer's®)
* 1 cup (240 ml) + 1 tablespoon (15 ml) water
* Measuring spoons
* Two glass bowls or other containers
* Measuring cup
* Spoons or stirrers
* Food coloring (optional)

1 Put the borax in one of the bowls or containers. Add 1 cup (240 ml) of water and stir until the borax dissolves.

If you want, you can color the mixture with food coloring. Mix in one drop each of several different colors to get the grossest-looking results.

2 In the other container, stir together 1 tablespoon (15 ml) of glue with 1 tablespoon (15 ml) of water. Stir until the mixture is completely blended.

3 Add just 1 tablespoon (15 ml) of the borax solution to the glue mixture. Stir until everything is completely mixed, with no lumps. Now you can take the mixture out and knead it. You've got slimy putty!

CAUTION: Do not get borax in your mouth or eyes! It can make you sick!

4 Experiment with your slimy putty. It has some pretty weird properties!

Roll it into a ball. Does it bounce?

Let the ball sit for a minute by itself. What happens?

! **Well, it shouldn't have to be said, but don't squash your slime putty into your hair, clothes, upholstery, or the carpet.**

Pull the putty slowly, and it stretches like bubblegum. Yank it hard, and it breaks.

To add grossness, roll the ball of putty along the kitchen floor under the front of the refrigerator and see what kinds of disgusting bits it picks up. (WARNING: If you do this, do it last. You'll never get the putty clean again.)

CLEANUP:
Be sure to clean the bowls, measuring cups, and spoons with dish soap and water before the goo dries on them. When you're done with the slimy putty, throw it away in the trash.

You may notice a similarity between slimy putty and a certain material sold inside a plastic egg. That stuff acts the same way, but it's made of slightly different ingredients.

BEHIND THE SLIME

Like Miracle Glop (p. 38), slimy putty is a polymer, made of long chainlike molecules. Polymer molecules in the white glue are cross-linked, or bound together, in a chemical reaction with the borax. The web of polymer molecules traps water, giving the putty its gooey texture. Slime putty has less water in it than runny slime does, which gives it a stiffer texture.

The SOAP BLOB Monster

Make an ordinary bar of soap swell into an enormous, monstrous blob!

There's nothing dangerous in this experiment, *but you DO need adult permission to use the microwave.* The experiment won't hurt the oven, but it will make everything smell like soap. And your favorite adult assistant would probably enjoy watching the spectacular results!

You'll need:

* 1 hand-size bar of Ivory® soap (No substitutions! No other kind of soap will work.)
* Paper plate (or a microwave-safe plate)
* Microwave oven
* Permission to use the microwave
* Marshmallows (optional)
* Adult assistant (optional)

1 Put the bar of soap on the plate. Put the plate in the microwave.

You can use a regular, microwave-safe plate instead of the paper one. You'll just have to clean some soap off afterward.

2 Set the microwave to cook for 2 minutes at high power.

Depending on your microwave, you might need to give it more or less time.

3 Press the start button.

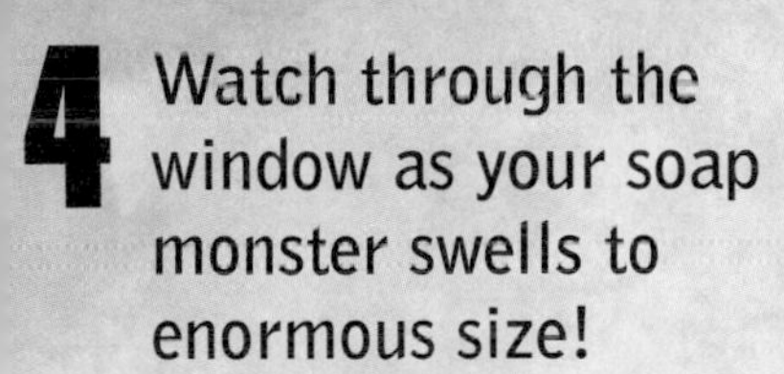

4 Watch through the window as your soap monster swells to enormous size!

CAUTION: The blob of foam will be very hot!

5 If your microwave oven doesn't have a window, you'll see the giant blob of soap foam at the end when you open the door. But be quick! It will start shrinking as soon as the oven shuts off.

BEHIND THE GROSS

Microwave ovens work by causing the water molecules in food to vibrate. The faster the molecules vibrate, the hotter the food gets. Like all soaps, Ivory soap contains water. Unlike other soaps, the Ivory bar is filled with tiny air spaces, like microscopic bubbles. When the water in the soap heats up, it turns to steam. The steam pressure expands the air spaces, breaking down the thin walls between them and swelling the bar into a monster blob of foam.

RADIO COOKING

Microwave ovens cook with electromagnetic waves, a form of energy that includes radio waves, light waves, X-rays, and cosmic rays. The oven puts out radio waves that can pass through objects like popcorn, TV dinners, and bars of soap. The oven's waves have the specific wavelength and frequency that causes water molecules to vibrate.

For extra grossness, try the same experiment with several marshmallows. (Don't use the same plate you used for the soap!) Marshmallows are smaller, so you won't have to cook them as long as the soap. The time depends on your microwave. (Try 30 seconds to a minute.) If the outside of the marshmallows starts to turn brown, turn the microwave off immediately, or you'll have a burned mess. Don't touch the marshmallows right away—they will be very hot. But once they cool, you can eat them.

Soda FOUNTAIN

Candies dropped in a bottle of cola create a sloppy geyser of mess!

CAUTION:
Do this experiment outside. It's very, very messy. And unless you're a fan of cleaning up messes, set the soda bottle on the ground, not on a sidewalk or a deck.

You'll need:

* 2-liter bottle of DIET cola (Get the cheapest stuff you can find. You won't be drinking it, so the taste doesn't matter.)
* Roll of Mentos® candy (any flavor)
* Letter-sized sheet of paper
* Tape
* Small, flat piece of cardboard

1 Don't open the candy yet! Roll the sheet of paper into a tube around the roll of Mentos. Tape it so it holds its tube shape. It should be just big enough to let the Mentos package slide out easily. Test it to make sure. Set the empty tube aside.

2 Place the cola bottle upright on the ground and take the lid off.

3 Open the roll of Mentos candy. Holding the flat piece of cardboard over one end of your paper tube, load the tube with all the candies from the package.

Mentos

4 Holding the tube of candies upright on the cardboard, place the cardboard and the candies on top of the mouth of the cola bottle. Line it up so that when you slip the cardboard out of the way, the candies will slide down into the bottle.

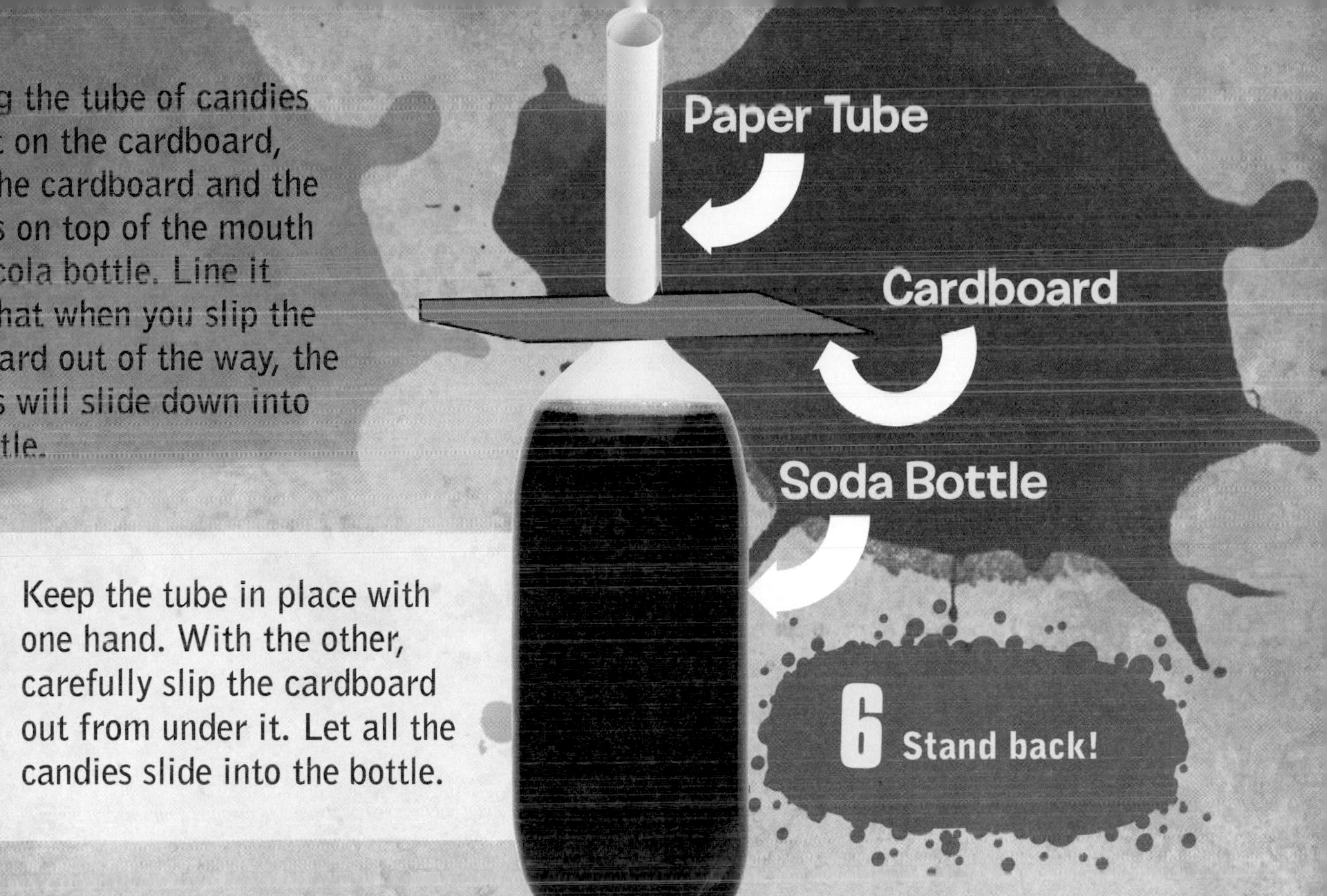

5 Keep the tube in place with one hand. With the other, carefully slip the cardboard out from under it. Let all the candies slide into the bottle.

6 Stand back!

Variations

Now that you've got the basics down, you can do some experimenting. A bottle of soda is only good for one geyser, so you'll need to use a fresh bottle each time. Which method gives you the tallest geyser and the biggest mess? Write down your results.

- **Try using regular cola instead of sugar-free. Is there a difference? (Regular cola contains corn syrup, which slows the bubble formation.)**
- **Try other flavors of soda.**
- **Try using Wint-O-Green® Life Savers® instead of Mentos candies.**
- **Try putting a tablespoon of salt in the bottle instead of candy. (Use a funnel.)**

BEHIND THE MESS

The fizz in cola comes from carbon dioxide (CO_2) gas dissolved in the liquid. Putting a rough-surfaced object in the drink causes bubbles to form on the object's surface. Mentos candies are rough on the outside, so bubbles form around them. The candy coating also contains gum arabic, which makes bubbles form more easily. The candies create a huge number of bubbles all at once. More bubbles form around those bubbles, the pressure of gas inside the bottle rises quickly—and *VOOM!* It's fountain time!

Sour Milk FUN

It's a race against the clock (well, the calendar) in this milk-curdling contest!

If you don't want to make a special trip to the store, you can do this experiment using just one kind of milk, pasteurized or ultra-pasteurized, whichever you have at home. In that case, you'll need only two jars.

You'll need:

* Pasteurized milk (enough to fill two jars)
* Ultra-pasteurized milk (enough to fill two small jars)
* 4 small, clean jars with lids
* Tape (masking tape is best)
* Marker
* Refrigerator

1 Use the tape and marker to label your jars. For the full experiment, mark them this way:

- **Regular, warm**
- **Ultra, warm**
- **Ultra, cold**
- **Regular, cold**

(If you're just doing the two-jar experiment, you don't need to mark them.)

2 Add another label to all the jars that says:

Otherwise someone in your house could be in for a very nasty surprise.

3 Pour regular pasteurized milk into the jars marked "regular." Pour ultra-pasteurized milk into the jars marked "ultra." Make sure you have the same amount of milk in each jar. Don't put the lids on yet.

4 Leave the jars out of the refrigerator until the milk warms up to room temperature. This may take an hour or more.

5 Close the jars. Put the ones marked "cold" in the refrigerator. Put the ones marked "warm" in a warm place.

ULTRA, COLD

REGULAR, COLD

6 Take a look at the jars after two days. Hold them up to the light and swirl the milk around. Have there been any changes? Put them back and check again in a few days. Keep checking the jars every few days for a week or more. Which jar gets grossest fastest? Record the milk-souring results.

Bacteria reproduce more slowly when they're cold, so milk stays fresher longer in the fridge.

BEHIND THE GROSS

Bacteria make milk sour. Even the freshest carton of milk contains some of these microbes, and more get in after you open it. The bacteria get energy from lactose, a sugar found in milk. They get rid of waste in the form of lactic acid. As the bacteria reproduce, they give off more and more lactic acid, making the milk taste sour. Eventually, the acid curdles the milk, forming disgusting chunks and clumps.

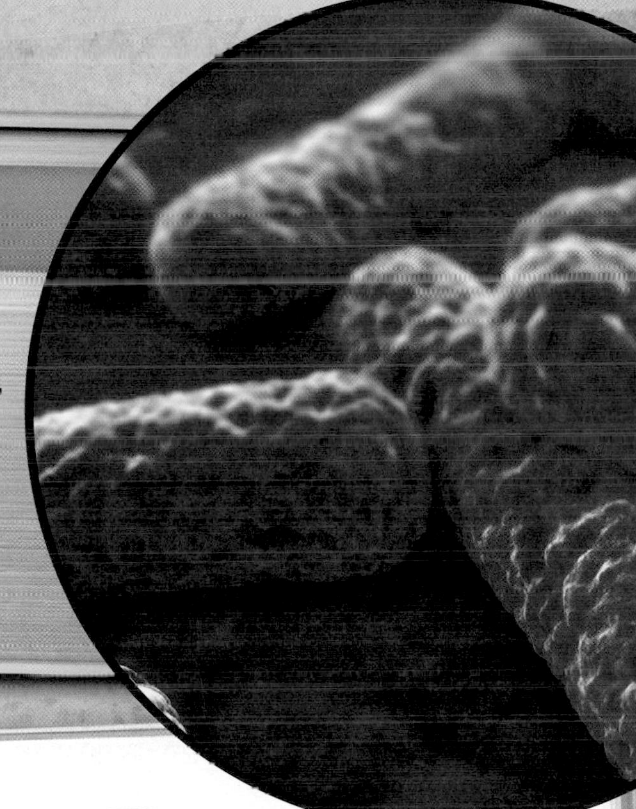

Bacteria busting

Pasteurized milk gets heated to 161°F (72°C) for at least 15 seconds, killing most bacteria. Ultra-pasteurized milk gets even hotter—at least 280°F (138°C) for at least 2 seconds. It's pretty much bacteria-free—until you open it, that is.

CLEANUP: At the end of this experiment, don't open the jars! Just throw them in the trash.

Stink RACE

CAUTION: This experiment involves sharp knives. An adult assistant is required.

Which smell travels fastest? Stink up the room with this smelly speed test!

You'll need:

* Adult assistant (REQUIRED)
* Volunteer smellers (at least one, but more are better)
* 4 or more containers with lids (Jars, leftover containers, or yogurt cups with lids work well.)
* Chair
* Stopwatch or clock with a second hand
* Paper and pencil or pen
* Electric fan (optional)
* 4 or more stinkers, such as these:
  - Crushed garlic clove (Put a clove of garlic on a plate or cutting board. Then, press down hard with the bottom of a glass to crush it.)
  - Chopped onion (Have an adult assistant chop it for you.)
  - A piece of overcooked broccoli or cabbage
  - A piece of burnt, crushed toast
  - A smelly, sweaty gym sock

1 Place one stinker in each container. (Use at least four stinkers and containers.) Close the containers, so the smells don't get out.

Crushed Garlic

Sweaty Sock

Overcooked Broccoli

Chopped Onion

Burnt Toast

2 **Set up your testing area. Put the chair at one end of a room in your housc. Put your stinker containers at the other end of the room.**

3 Prepare your sheet of paper. Write the names of the stinkers across the top of the paper. Write the name(s) of your volunteer smeller(s) down the side.

	Crushed Garlic	Sweaty Sock	Overcooked Broccoli	Chopped Onion	Burnt Toast
Volunteer Smeller #1					
Volunteer Smeller #2					
Volunteer Smeller #3					

4 Call your first victim—er, volunteer. Have the volunteer sit in the chair. Explain what you're going to do: You're going to open the containers one at a time. Then, time how long it takes for your volunteer to smell what's inside.

There are two ways you can run the experiment. You can tell your volunteer what smell to expect, or you can keep the smell a secret and have the volunteer identify the stink when he or she smells it.

5 Go across the room to your containers. For each container, one at a time:

- Open the lid and start the stopwatch or notice the position of the second hand on the clock.
- Time how long it takes for the smell to reach the smeller. Write the time on your record sheet.
- Put the lid on the container.
- Wait at least five minutes for the smell to clear out. Use a fan (if you have one) to help clear the air.

Burnt Toast

Sweaty Sock

Overcooked Broccoli

6 If you have more than one volunteer smeller, repeat the whole test with each volunteer.

Chopped Onion

Crushed Garlic

7 Analyze your data. Which smells were detected the fastest? Were there time differences between the different smellers?

BEHIND THE STINK

We smell smells when scent molecules go up our noses and get detected by special smell-detecting nerve cells. When you open each container, scent molecules from the stinker inside start to spread out into the air. The amount of time it takes your volunteers to notice the smell depends on two things: how long it takes the molecules to travel across the room, and what concentration (the number of smell molecules per billion air molecules) the cells need to detect the smell.

Worm RANCH

Round 'em up and head 'em out! Watch earthworms tunnel in a miniature worm ranch!

CAUTION: This experiment requires an adult assistant.

You'll need:

* Adult assistant (REQUIRED)
* Clear (not green) 2-liter plastic soda bottle
* Potting soil (enough to almost fill the bottle)
* 2 cups (480 ml) grass clippings or dry leaves
* Water
* Small sponge (new, never used)
* Sheet of dark-colored construction paper, at least 8 ½ x 14 inches (22 x 36 cm). If you only have 8 ½ x 11 inch (22 x 28 cm) paper, you'll need two sheets.
* An old nylon stocking or one leg from a pair of pantyhose (or a piece of other "breathable" fabric)
* Scissors
* Tape
* Rubber band

Cut Here!

1 Have your adult assistant help you cut off the top of the soda bottle. Cut it just below the place where it starts to curve inward to the neck, about where the top of the label is. Remove the label and wash the inside of the bottle with soap and water. Rinse it well.

2 Fill the bottle ¾ full with potting soil. Add the grass clippings or dry leaves (crumble the leaves first), and mix it all together, adding just enough water to make the mixture damp but not muddy.

3 Cut off a small square of sponge, about 2 inches (5 cm) on a side. Get it wet, squeeze it out, and place it on top of the dirt.

4 Round up four or five earthworms (no more than that). You can look for them outside in the dirt, or aboveground after it rains, or you can ask someone you know who has a backyard worm bin. If you can't find any free worms, you can buy them from a garden store or a nursery.

Worm Ranch continues on the next page.

5 Get your hands wet before handling the worms. Put the worms in the worm ranch and cover them with more grass clippings or leaves.

6 Slip the stocking or the piece of fabric over the top of the bottle to keep the worms from escaping. Use a rubber band to holc it in place.

7 Wrap the construction paper all the way around the bottle to cover the whole thing, and then tape it in place. Tape the paper to itself, not the bottle. You'll want to be able to slip it on and off.

8 Place your worm ranch in a cool place out of the sun. Keep the sponge damp—check it every two days. After a week, slide off the construction paper and look at the tunnels your worm herd has made!

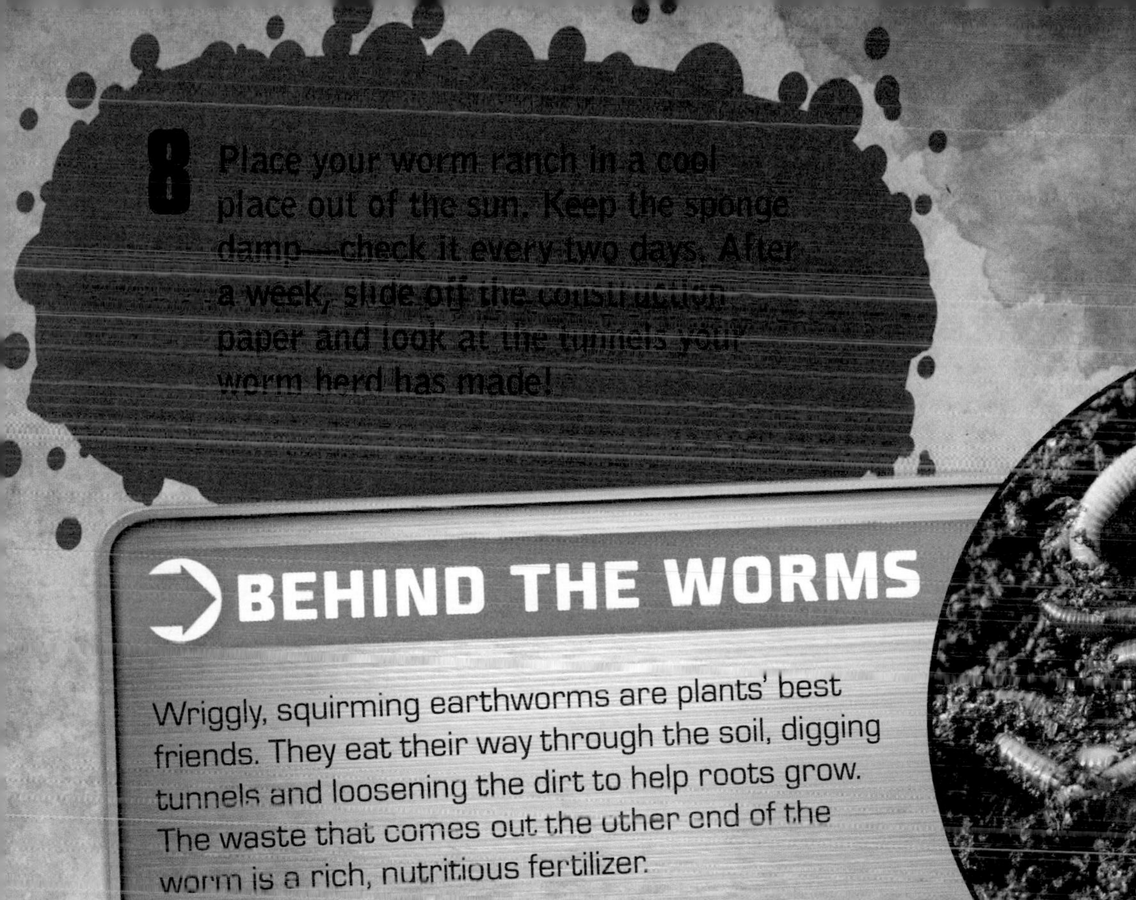

BEHIND THE WORMS

Wriggly, squirming earthworms are plants' best friends. They eat their way through the soil, digging tunnels and loosening the dirt to help roots grow. The waste that comes out the other end of the worm is a rich, nutritious fertilizer.

MORE WORMINESS

You can keep your worm ranch for a couple of weeks, but *no longer than that.* Feed the worms plant scraps like potato peels, lettuce, leaves, and grass clippings. Remove and replace any moldy food. Don't forget to put the construction paper back on the bottle after you observe the worms—they like dark spaces.

After no more than two weeks, release your worms into the wild. Backyards and gardens are perfect places for them.

One acre (.4 ha) of land can contain as many as a million earthworms!

Certificate of Grossness

____

(name)

having completed the course of Gross Science experiments, is herewith granted the title Youth Experimenter and Critical Concept Haver (officially abbreviated YECCH). For scientific work that goes above and beyond ordinary grossness—and for delving into topics like maggots, mold, mummies, and mucus—we congratulate you! Go forth and be gross!

Alice Phlegm, GPhD
(Doctor of Gross Philosophy)

Stuart Germworthy
(GD, Doctor of Grossness)